Old Haddington

by Craig Statham

The Happy Valley is situated on the St Lawrence Burn in the middle of the Knowes. The roof of Braeheads (which was once the last house on the route heading west out of Haddington) can be seen in the background.

First published in the United Kingdom, 2007,
by Stenlake Publishing Ltd.
www.stenlake.co.uk
ISBN 9781840333909

References

I used too many books and ephemeral documents for them all to be listed here. Suffice to say that all are available to read at the Local History Centre in Newton Port, Haddington. Anyone undertaking further reading might want to start with the four *Statistical Accounts of East Lothian*, John Martine's excellent *Reminiscences of the Royal Burgh of Haddington* (published in 1883), Gray and Jamieson's *A Short History of Haddington* (published in 1944) and James Miller's *The Lamp of Lothian* (published in 1844).

Acknowledgements

I must thank staff at the East Lothian Council Libraries and Museums for kindly allowing me to use a number of photographs. Thanks must also go to George Angus and Jack Tully-Jackson, both of whom dated images and corrected several narrative errors on my part. The publishers wish to thank the following for permission to reproduce images in this book: East Lothian Museums Service for pages 9, 11, 14 and 16; East Lothian Library Service for pages 15 and 40, John Hamilton for page 43 (top); and Craig Statham for pages 6 and 56.

Situated one mile west of Haddington is the old leper colony of St Lawrence House. It existed as early as 1366 when a payment was made to the 'Master of the Hospital' and there was still a hospital in a 'plain two-storey building' in 1889. The houses shown here were erected in 1906, although those on the right have now been demolished. The area has been host to at least two great armies – Cromwell camped here on his journey from Leith to Dunbar in 1650, and in 1745 Sir John Cope used the area as a camp for his troops the day before the Battle of Prestonpans. In later years excavations in the area found the skeletons of thousands of people who had died of leprosy.

INTRODUCTION

The burgh of Haddington is situated in rural surroundings 17 miles east of Edinburgh. But for all its solitude from the urban bustle of Scotland's capital, this relatively small town can lay claim to a long, rich and diverse history. When the area was first settled is unknown, but its written history begins in the twelfth century. It is likely that it was around this time that the town had burgh status conferred upon it, most likely by King David I. A further royal link occurred in 1198 when the future King Alexander II was born in a palace in the town, believed to be roughly in the area the County Buildings occupy today. The town's journey through the following centuries are littered with catastrophes – both man-made and natural. It was burned at least three times during English raids, and flooded at least four.

Throughout the town's history there has been a slow but steady population growth. In 1789 the population stood at 2,567. By 1835, including Nungate, it had risen to 3,751 and a century later it was 4,405. Two major changes occurred during this period – the number of children (under 15 years of age) more than halved and there was a notable rise in the number of aged residents. In the twentieth century the incorporation of the Glasgow overspill from the 1950s onwards, tied with the burgh now being in easy commuting distance of Edinburgh, led to a population boom and by 2001 the population stood at 8,851.

The town is surrounded by farmland and agriculture has played an integral role in its development. In 1789 it was noted that virtually the whole parish was highly cultivated arable land. At this time, when Haddington was home to Scotland's largest grain market, there were around 30 farms, those near the town being rented at between £3 and 50s per acre. This figure decreased enormously if the farm was more than three miles from the town. Around 50 years later it was noted that around 97.3% of land in the parish was under cultivation, while improvements in farming techniques (drainage and crop rotation) were making the soil more productive. The town housed some of the farm servants who were paid in kind and were said to be in a 'thriving condition'. The grain and cattle markets closed around the 1960s and production on the surrounding 40 farms is now primarily of wheat, barley and oilseed rape.

Although it could be argued that agriculture is the foundation upon which Haddington flourished, its industry should not be overlooked. The proximity of the town to the River Tyne has ensured that industry has, for many centuries, played a significant role in its success. In 1681 Colonel Sir James Stanfield opened a fine woollen cloth manufactory on the lands later known as Amisfield. In 1835 Thomas Bernard opened a distillery near West Mill which was to remain in business until 1992. And, taking advantage of the Tyne waters, the West Mill was home to numerous industries through the years, most notably tweed making. Industry also thrived on the Nungate side of the river with the Gimmers Mills, the tannery and the Bermaline Mill, the latter still making flour today. In the twentieth century a number of businesses were founded that proved highly successful. Richard Baillie, a contractor who receives a number of mentions in this book, completed large-scale demolition and building works from 1902 through to 1962. Kilspindie Knitwear employed a number of local people from 1917 until its demise in 1991, and over the last 25 years industries – albeit hugely different from those only a few years previously – continued to be drawn to the town. Ranco arrived in 1956 and, after a number of name changes (most recently to Lothian Electrical Machines Ltd), is still hiring local people today. In 1980 Mitsubishi Electronics arrived, making mostly televisions for continental Europe. At its peak it employed around 500 people, but sadly closed down in 1999.

Haddington is believed to be the birthplace of the religious reformer John Knox, who played a central role in introducing early educational reform to Scotland, and it should perhaps come as little surprise that education is an important part of the town's history. Schools were certainly in existence in Haddington prior to the Protestant Reformation. An English school was created around 1750 to join the Grammar School. In the latter half of the eighteenth century the Halyburton sisters were running a girls' school out of Sandybed House, while at this time the town had a Circulating Library. A Mathematical School was opened in 1809. In 1817 John Gray, a minister at Aberlady, bequested his library to the town. Samuel Brown's Itinerating Libraries were based in the town from 1817 and Brown also helped create a Scientific Society in the town in the same year and, in the 1820s, a School of Arts (also known as the Mechanic's Institute), where lectures were given. In the 1870s St Mary's Roman Catholic School was opened and, in 1879, the Knox Institute (now known as Knox Academy). Today, Haddington has a single library service that covers the whole region. As well as its local branches it delivers to the housebound, to homes and hospitals, and to schools. St Mary's Roman Catholic Primary and Knox Academy continue to flourish, the latter being fed by Haddington Infant School and King's Meadow Primary, while these have been joined by the independent Compass School. Additionally, lifelong learners can augment their skills by taking classes at the further education college at Alderston House.

It is perhaps fitting, in the town of Samuel Smiles, the author of *Self Help*, that self-help has played a major role in the lives of Haddington's inhabitants. The earliest examples of this, at least on a large scale, were the trade incorporations. But one had to be a skilled artisan to join these and smaller benevolent groups were formed by those who were excluded. These included the Mutual Assurance Society and the Female Society. By the nineteenth century the self-help societies began to grow in size, thus creating a better financial safety net. Haddington had long had one of these larger societies – the Free Gardeners, formed in 1676, and in the 1800s it was joined by the Oddfellows and the Foresters. Also notable at this time was the creation of the Haddington Co-operative Society. By the 1950s, however, the effect of the pre-Great War and post-Second World War reforms had all but ended the need for many of these societies. Of the early societies, only the Freemasons still exist in anything like their original form. Today's societies are founded in the desire for social interaction rather than financial well being, thus many of the groups are primarily a place where people can meet and chat, such as the Haddington Lunch and Social Club or the Haddington Remembered Group.

Today, Haddington is a thriving, vibrant community founded on a rich history where industry, agriculture, education, industry and self-help have all played an integral role. Importantly, they continue to do so.

Haddington Station was opened in 1846 by the North British Railway Company. It included a goods siding, a shed, a turntable for locomotives and a booking office, and the first station agent was C.H. Davidson. The station was situated to the west of the town and in those early days passengers could be carried to the George Hotel in a 'dusty little [horse-drawn] omnibus'. The floods of 1948 caused the booking office to be closed and it was temporarily replaced by an old railway carriage which housed both the ticket office and waiting room. Passenger services ended in December the following year. The track, like so many others in the Lothians, is now a walking and cycling path. This photograph was taken around the turn of the century, while the one on the left probably dates from the 1930s.

The Ferguson Monument, a well-known Haddington landmark. In 1830 the Whig Party, having been asked to form a government by King George IV, proposed reforming the voting system to end the problem of rotten burghs and fixed elections. But first they needed to take power. At the 1831 election Haddington, North Berwick, Dunbar, Jedburgh and Lauder were combined as a single parliamentary seat. Haddington and Jedburgh supported the Whig candidate, Robert Steuart, while North Berwick and Dunbar supported the Tory candidate, Sir Adolphus John Dalrymple. The vote at Lauder hung in the balance and a plan was hatched by local Whig supporters to ensure the election of Robert Steuart. On the morning of the election men from Haddington and throughout the Borders 'carried off' Baillie Simpson, who was likely to vote Tory, in a post-chaise and as a result Robert Steuart won by one vote. Due to the 'kidnapping', later called the 'Lauder Raid', Steuart's election was nullified, although he did serve long enough to vote for the Reform Bill, which was passed by a single vote. After the Reform Act was passed in 1832, power in Haddingtonshire stayed with the Tories (as Steuart was replaced by Dalrymple), although in the election of 1835 it was wrested from them by a new Whig candidate, Robert Ferguson of Raith. His undistinguished tenure lasted only two years when he lost to the Tory candidate, Lord Ramsay, in 1837. Nonetheless, after Ferguson's death in 1840, his services to the county were recognised with the erection of a 45-foot-high whinstone memorial column - costing £650 raised by subscription - on the corner of Knox Place and Station Road. The architect was Robert Forrest. Around the base are figures representing Justice, Geology, Art and Agriculture. An inscription describes Ferguson as, 'a kind landlord, a liberal dispenser of wealth' although some evidently disagreed. One anonymous observer wrote, 'It is rather silly . . . that in the county town of Knox, Rennie, Meikle, Jane Welsh, Balfour, and other famous men and women with some claim to our remembrance, the most eye-catching memorial (and the finest site) should be reserved for a nobody.' The column was unveiled on 2 June 1843.

Looking down on the town from the tower of the West Church, around 1920. Court Street runs up to the Town House where it splits into Market Street on the left and High Street on the right.

This photograph shows the Town House in 1923. It was designed by William Adam in 1742, but building work did not begin until six years later. It was an expansive structure – 60 feet x 36 feet, set over three floors – housing the town council, the sheriff court and the town jail. By the mid-twentieth century a report noted that 'the jail is not of a good construction. It is not supplied with water, the cells are badly ventilated, and there is no proper provision for cleanliness'. It is unlikely that it was still being used for prisoners by that time, although the comment gives some indication of conditions when it was in use and it also frequently failed to cope with the number of prisoners. This is likely the reason an extension was added to the west side of the building in 1788. The first steeple lasted until 1831 when it was replaced by the one shown here. It was planned by James Gillespie Graham and, 170 feet high, was built by the mason James M'Watt. In the post-Second World War years there were calls for the building to be demolished as it was riddled with dry rot and was causing a bottleneck due to the rise in traffic. After speaking to the architect Peter Whiston, who argued that it was not beyond salvage, John McVie, the Town Clerk, called for it to be restored in time for the Queen's Coronation in 1953. The refurbished building was opened by Mary, Princess Royal (daughter of King George V). Three months later Queen Elizabeth, in Haddington for a short visit with Prince Philip, learned that her aunt had opened the building and was given an unscheduled tour. The building is now used primarily for meetings and seminars.

The German invasion of Poland in 1939 led to an exodus of young Polish men (one of whom was the author's grandfather) who made their way west by any means they could, mainly to France. With the fall of France in 1940 they descended on Britain and were soon sent to Scotland. Their first two years were spent 'defending' the east coast from Burntisland to Montrose. When General Maczek's 1st Polish Armoured Division was formed in 1942, the men were sent to towns throughout Scotland. The 10th Mounted Rifles were based in Haddington, primarily at Amisfield. The Poles' old-world manners won them many friends and a Scottish-Polish Society was set up in the town. In 1943, at a ceremony in Lady Kitty's Garden, the town gave a flag and scroll to the regiment – the flag was presented by Alan Mills of No. 1 Haddington Scout Troop – and in return they received a plaque made of Aberdeen granite. Soon after, the regiment left for England for training before heading to Normandy in August 1944 and Amisfield was then used as a prisoner–of–war camp for Germans and Ukranians. This photograph shows the regiment's tanks in Court Street. Although the Poles who were integrated into the Royal Air Force have gathered greater plaudits in recent years, the soldiers certainly played their part, helping to close the Falaise Gap and liberating many Belgian and Dutch towns. Many returned to become UK citizens after the war.

In 1786 Royal Mail coaches replaced horseback deliveries of mail from Edinburgh to London. The Old Post Road, along which the mail was carried, ran directly through Haddington and the town's post office was based in Sidegate, opposite Haddington House. In 1818 it moved to the Custom Stone behind the George Hotel, and it was here that the mail coaches changed their horses. At this time mail was only delivered to the town, and from there to outlying villages by 'runners', the equivalent of modern postmen. In May 1909 a new post office, designed by Mr Brown of Aberlady, was opened in Court Street and was described as 'commodious and imposing', although some complained that it 'cannot be said to be in the business centre of the town.' The office's three telegraph messengers are pictured outside the building soon after its opening and it continues to serve as the town's post office today. The post box, to the right of the lady, remains in the same place.

Co-operative societies were formed throughout Scotland in the nineteenth century. The aim of the founders was to improve the lot of the local working men and their families by providing quality, affordable foodstuffs. In some cases they even provided cheap housing for their members. They also provided a healthy social outlet and many choirs were formed and plays and shows put on. The Haddington Co-operative Society was formed in 1867. As well as owning shops in the town, it provided services to those in outlying areas by opening branches in places such as North Berwick and Gifford. In 1936 it merged with the Tranent Society and three years later the Dunbar and West Barns Society was incorporated to form the East Lothian Co-operative Society. It merged with the Borders Regional Co-op in 1992, and there was a further merger with the Angus society in 1998 to form Lothian, Borders and Angus Co-operative Society Ltd. This photograph shows staff at the rear of the Lodge Street premises around 1914.

A photograph from around 1916, looking west along Market Street towards the Town House. Charles Bruce, whose shop is on the right, is a name that will be well known to any collector of East Lothian postcards as he published many of those featured within this book, including this one which has his name printed on its back. Bruce opened his stationer's shop around 1890 and it remained at No. 22 until 1928, when it was being run by members of his family. On the opposite side of the road the car is parked at Richard Baillie's Central Garage.

Jane Welsh was born in Haddington in 1801 and spent her early years in this house in Lodge Street, which – thanks to the efforts of the Lamp of Lothian Collegiate Trust – remains much the same as it was in her day. She was a very academic child, becoming dux of St Anne's School, and her intellect drew her to the writer Thomas Carlyle, who she married in 1826. By 1830 the couple were living in London and associating with the likes of Dickens, Thackeray and Tennyson. In 1866, when travelling in her carriage, Jane stopped to allow her dog a walk. It was immediately struck by another carriage and, shocked, Jane suffered a heart attack and died. Her husband had her body sent to Haddington and she was buried in St Mary's Churchyard.

Friendly societies were organisations set up to financially protect their members, who – during their working lives – would pay a regular fee to the society. If they fell ill and could not work, or funeral costs needed to be met, they or their family would reap the benefit. One such society was the Ancient Fraternity of Free Gardeners of East Lothian, formed before 1676 and the earliest known Free Gardener Lodge. In 1782, at a cost of £105, it purchased this property in Market Street – naming it the Gardeners' Arms. The upper floors served as the Lodge's meeting hall and headquarters, while the remainder was let as accommodation and a public house. In 1888 it was sold for £450 and, soon after this photograph was taken in the late 1800s, its three floors were converted to two and its frontage decorated with the symbols of the society – a square, compass and pruning knife. The society was wound up in 1952, but its minute books, regalia and a range of other items have survived. In its early years members had to actively practice gardening, but non-practicing members were soon admitted. They undertook Masonic-type rituals and would march annually through the town. They were not averse to pledging their political allegiance, joining a procession to celebrate the election of the reforming Whig Robert Steuart in 1831.

The Loyal Tyneside Lodge of Oddfellows, No. 3429, was founded on 24 January 1843. It soon prospered and in less than 20 years had its own hall in Brown Street. In 1862 the hall was renovated and 'painted in a style of chaste elegance'. By 1860 it had funds of £2,974 16*s*, and in its 17 years had distributed almost £2,500 to members from its Sick and Assurance Scheme. In 1873 a junior section was formed. Social events were also a high priority and back issues of the *Haddingtonshire Courier* reveal a society that frequently travelled out of town on away days and organised events within the town's public houses. This photograph shows the lodge's shooting team and the trophy in the foreground is probably the Friendly Societies' Trophy for which the Oddfellows competed annually against the Freemasons and the Foresters. They are known to have won in 1903 and 1910. Not all was smooth sailing for the Lodge however. In 1866 they clashed with their governing body, the Manchester Unity, over payments to members, and nine years later – in another incident – a member was thrown out of the society and then petitioned the sheriff to be reinstated. But despite such occurrences, the lodge continued to survive well into the twentieth century.

The last of Haddington's major friendly societies to be established was the Court Lamp of Lothian, No. 4793 of the Ancient Order of Foresters, formed in 1865. Despite being founded by only 14 members, the Court soon began to grow. Having spent its formative years holding meetings at the Freemasons' Hall, in June 1878 the Court opened its own hall in Hardgate (which can be seen on the left of photograph on the next page), designed by local man Francis Farquharson (who also designed the Corn Exchange) at a cost of £1,500. (Ironically, in November 1952 the Freemasons moved into the Foresters' Hall after they left their earlier premises in Lodge Street.) The Court also opened a junior section – Court Jane Welsh. Many friendly societies allied themselves to famous historical or religious figures. For example, the Free Gardeners created rituals and social events based on the biblical stories of Adam and Eve and the Garden of Eden. For the Foresters this figure was Robin Hood; Lincoln green was a colour frequently used by them and some members even dressed up as Robin Hood on social occasions. At Court Lamp of Lothian's first anniversary celebrations member James Nicholson wore 'a hunting tunic of Lincoln green velvet, slashed with gold and ermine, reached to the knee. Spotless tights, and buff buskin boots . . . a white pointed-lace collar, white gauntlets, and green velvet cocked hat . . . a lofty nodding plume . . . [and was] armed with a long-pointed hunting spear [and] silver-mounted horn.' The Court finally closed down in 1988 but the hall still survives and, although now owned by Lodge St John Kilwinning, No. 57 of the Freemasons, the symbol of the Court – a stag's head – can still be seen on the wall above the door. Only Musselburgh's Court Pride of the Esk still survives in East Lothian.

From as early as 1550, and possibly earlier, Haddington's 'industry' was controlled by nine trade incorporations – the baxters, hammermen, masons, wrights, fleshers, cordiners, skinners, tailors and weavers – known collectively as the Convenor Court of Haddington. They ensured that any goods coming into the town would have to meet certain quality standards and those bringing it in would have to pay a fee. In the wake of the American and French revolutions, government paranoia about potential rebellions led to them introducing laws that forbade meetings of groups of men. This led to the gradual demise of the trade incorporations in the nineteenth century and their eventual replacement by friendly societies. One of the most well known of these in Haddington was the Carters' Society – its members being the men who transported goods by horse. Many of their aims were similar to the trade incorporations; they even carried on the tradition of holding an annual fair – called the 'Carters' Fair'. This had its roots in the fairs granted to the town in 1624 by James VI and ratified nine years later by Charles I. These included the eight-day-long St Peter's Fair in July and the Michaelmas Fair in September. On the day of the Carters' Fair a procession, including the town's drummer and piper, would be led by 'My Lord' on a decorated horse. He would dismount at the burgh school and request

of the rector that the students be given a holiday in order to watch the horse races, which for many years were run from Smail's Pond to St Lawrence House. On their way along High Street the riders proceeded around the Market Cross, from which was hung a cat in a barrel, and they would attempt to burst open the barrel. Foot races were run from the Ball Alley, over the Nungate Bridge, along Ford Road and back through the Tyne, and the winner received 10*s*. At another time horse races were held in Plum Park with the winning rider yelling towards the finishing line, 'Bat the drum! Bat the drum! Am first! Am first!' In the evening a dance was held in the council room of the Town House. The last Carters' Fair was held in 1858, and the society was wound up the following year, a victim of the growing popularity of the railway for transporting goods. However, the society did continue on in another form as the Haddington Carters' and Merchants' Association, and out of the old Carters' Fair was born the town's Gala Day. These photographs show the event around 1912. Admission at that time would have been 6*d* for adults and 3*d* for children, plus 2*s* 6*d* per carriage.

The 'My Lord' pictured here in 1909 at Under Langside Park, while leading a Carters' Fair procession, is believed to be William Murray, a local lawyer. Born around 1865, he attended Watson's College and Edinburgh University. He returned to Haddington some years later and acquired a solicitors' business. He was well respected and held a number of notable positions outwith his law work, including editor of the *Scottish Estate Factors' Magazine*, local agent of the Union Bank of Scotland, secretary of the East Lothian Farmers' Union, chairman of the Haddington Combined School Board, and Honorary Treasurer of the Town Council, among others. During the Great War he was the County Food Controller and this work earned him an MBE. After a long illness, he died in 1924. His funeral, at Haddington Churchyard, was conducted according to Masonic ritual, and the list of attendees was impressive.

The horse-drawn delivery van of the butcher Joseph Reid, who had a shop in Court Street from 1910 to 1924. It is likely this photograph was taken during Gala Day celebrations. Reid's old premises are still in use as a butcher's shop, occupied by Colin D. Peat & Son.

In direct competition with Reid would have been the butcher's business of George Pringle, based at No. 17 Market Street. He opened his business around 1887.

From around the twelfth century many towns in Scotland were given burgh status which gave them the right to trade, and market crosses were the symbolic of this right. They were erected in the main trading area and traders would gather around them to sell their wares. The earliest ones were made of wood – unsurprisingly, none survive – and these were replaced by stone structures. It is not known when Haddington's first market cross, also known as the 'mercat croce' or 'the goat', was erected, but in his history of the town John Martine has argued that it was probably in the reign of David I in the twelfth century. This would certainly fit in with what was happening in similar towns at this time. Little is known of the cross's history over the next 500 years and it is likely that it was replaced at least once. In 1693 a stone cross was erected by John Jack, a mason, for 'fourtie pund Scots'. Its 12-feet-high shaft was as 'thick as a man's waist' and topped by a unicorn. It stood for 118 years until two local youths bet a visiting English artisan that he could not climb to the top of the structure. He succeeded, but the cross collapsed. It was replaced by a wooden one which Martine called a 'worn fir stick', but this was burned down around 1881 (bonfires were commonplace at celebrations held in the town). The present cross, a gift from Daniel and John Bernard of Holme House, has stood since 1928. Twenty-five feet high and topped by a goat, its prominent position – jutting into the road of High Street – has been the cause of much contention, due to the rise in traffic over the years. In 1963 councillors discussed moving it, the front of the Town House being one suggestion, but this never happened.

It is thanks in great part to the efforts of East Lothian's County Planning Officer, Frank Tindall, who was hired by the county in 1950, that Haddington today is not just another drab Scottish town dominated by concrete 'architecture'. Tindall fought to retain Haddington's historic architectural integrity and believed the town's tired landscape should be refurbished, rather than demolished and rebuilt. One of his first successes was to attach streetlights to the walls of buildings, throwing out 'a nice pale moonlight effect'. He was less successful in stopping the covering up of the setts in High Street with tarmac – his opposition almost cost him his job! His broader vision was finally realised when High Street was given a facelift by the Town Centre Refurbishment Scheme, which was the first of its kind in Scotland. By the 1950s many of the buildings in the town's High Street had become a dull buff colour and the architects Eric Hall and Partners were called in to create a colour scheme. Walls were painted a range of earth colours, and doors in bright colours, while windows were painted white and all architectural detail was highlighted in bright colour. Gold signs were erected above many shops. For example, Main the saddler fitted a golden horse above his door while both chemists added the traditional pestle and mortar. In October 1962 the Secretary of State for Scotland, Michael Noble, along with the town's Provost and Convenors, attended a ceremony in the town to mark the completion of the facelift and in 1969 the renewal and restoration of Haddington was rewarded when the town was designated an 'outstanding conservation area'.

WILLIAMSON & Co. DRAPERS & CLOTHIERS

Even Frank Tindall's efforts could not save all the town's streets being changed beyond recognition. Brown Street, for example, bears little resemblance today to this photograph taken around 1905. The street was originally known as Strumpet Lane and was then renamed George Inn Wynd before being given its present name.

'his late-sixteenth or early-seventeenth century building in Hardgate is commonly called Bothwell Castle, due to the fact that the Earl of Bothwell fled o it in 1559 to escape the Earl of Arran and Lord James Stewart. But the name is something of a misnomer. In its prime it was, at best, a large house, and t is perhaps more appropriate to call it by its actual title – Sandybed House. From around 1762 it was used as a school for young girls and by the eginning of the twentieth century it was described by MacGibbon and Ross, noted architectural authors, as 'one of the best specimens of old Scottish lomestic architecture left in Haddington.' In 1928 it came up for public roup and was purchased by Richard Baillie of Pencaitland. It was Baillie's ntention to re-roof and restore what was, by then, a ruin. He promised to offer it rent-free to Haddington's spinsters, and also to house within it a nuseum, but the council's Works Committee scuppered this plan by requesting that he demolish it 'before it [falls] down.' And so, in 1951, the company hat had demolished Amisfield House also knocked down another of the town's buildings of antiquity.

Although a plaque on the front of Haddington House in the town's Sidegate bears the date 1680, it is likely that the rear was built prior to this. Beside the date are the initials of the owners of the time – Alexander Maitland, a local burgess, and his wife, Katherine Cunningham. This photograph, with the house on the right, was taken around 1890. By the 1940s a four-acre orchard at the rear was no longer in use and was acquired by the Earl of Wemyss for the East Lothian Antiquarian and Field Naturalists' Society. Financial aid for its restoration came from the Stanley Smith Garden Trust and was overseen by Sir George Taylor and Sir David Lowe. The house itself, threatened with demolition, was purchased by the Lamp of Lothian Collegiate Trust (founded by the Duchess of Hamilton) in 1967. In 1969 it was restored by the architect Walter Schomberg Scott, and included rooms for community volunteers and for those studying to go to university. In 1994 it was put up for sale and the trust moved to Poldrate Mill. It is currently used as office space by East Lothian Council.

The Parish Church of St Mary the Virgin is Haddington's oldest and most spectacular structure. Built in the twelfth century, the 'Lamp of the Lothians', as it is also known, was the victim of many English attacks. The church that is present today is not the original structure; that was too small and so was rebuilt in 1365. By the late-eighteenth century it was in dire need of repair, with fears that the tower might collapse. Wooden beams (later replaced by iron rods) were put in place to divert disaster. Despite these precautions, fears continued about the state of the tower and the transepts, and in 1902 – around the time this photograph was taken – John Christie offered the minister, Dr Robert Nimmo Smith, £7,000 for restoration. But Christie died before the money changed hands and the repairs, which had proceeded as far as having the plans drawn up, could not be undertaken. In 1971, with money from Dr Smith's daughter, Hilda, along with donations from beneficiaries, £41,000 raised from the sale of four communion cups, and monies from fundraising events such as concerts by Yehudi Menuhin, restoration work began. Even the Victoria and Albert Museum lent a hand – donating a stained glass window from their collection. In the following years many further changes took place – a new organ was installed in 1990 and a set of eight bells was lifted into place in 1999. The church continues to flourish today.

The above photograph shows the western end of Church Street around 1910. The one opposite was taken around five years later. The rounded structure on the far left of the latter picture is Lady Kitty's Doocot. Viewed from the rear, in Lady Kitty's Garden, below the level of the wall, the base is actually of a square construction.

Church Street, Haddington.
Photo by: G. Bruce. Haddington.

Meadow Park, around 1910. At the end of the street is the gasworks which was erected in 1836. Gas had first come to the town fifteen years earlier when a Mr Nisbet used it to light his house and shop.

Between 1803 and 1805 Britain was at war with France and three sets of barracks were built in Haddington. The cavalry was housed around the area shown on the right of this photograph, known as Hope Park. James Miller, author of *The Lamp of Lothian*, called that time East Lothian's golden age, due to a growth in population which was a boon for the area's farmers. This photograph was taken in 1922. On the left is Robertson's orchard, and in the background is the County Lunatic Asylum. None of the barracks remain.

The County Lunatic Asylum opened in August 1866. The initial estimate of the cost was £6,000 for the main building and £1,500 for the outbuildings and grounds, although the actual costs were not recorded. Patients tended the gardens. The council also owned Alderston Farm and on weekdays around 20 to 25 patients could be seen walking to work there as they were a cheap labour force. The first governor was Mr Watson and the first matron a Miss Henderson. The building still survives today as Herdmanflat Hospital, an institution for people with mental health problems.

ohn Christie of Cowden took a great interest in the welfare of the young. To this end he began to open Female Industrial Homes (known as Christie Iomes) to house orphans. The first to open in Haddington was Tenterfield on Dunbar Road in 1898, shown here around 1920. After Christie's death in 902 Templedean, Carmendean, and a school adjoined to Tenterfield were opened by his trustees. The homes and school gave their girls a Christian ducation and skills that would serve them well in the workplace and as housewives. One 'old girl' noted, '[Mr Christie's helpers] moulded our lives, nd they will never know how far-reaching their influence for good has been. The bright memories of our girlhood will smooth the rough places of our uture.' The homes remained open until 1950 when a new building was erected at Newton Port. From that time Tenterfield was used as a local authority hildrens' home until 1992 and three years later it was converted into flats. But John Christie's benevolence towards the town did not end there and he ifted the town a steam fire engine. He also offered a sum of £7,000 to restore Haddington Parish Church (St Mary's) but his death meant that this proposal vas never undertaken. Indeed, it would be another 70 years before the church was finally restored.

As its name suggest, the lands of Monkrigg were originally owned by monks and some of the surrounding fields still bear appropriately religious names such as Upper and Lower Purgatory. The first owners of the estate in its modern form was the Hepburn family. Since then it has changed hands many times over the years. The building shown here was designed by William Burn in 1832 at the behest of the owner, Captain Keith, who later sold the house to George More for £16,000. More died in 1869 and the house passed to his uncle, James More. However, several prospective beneficiaries of the house were convinced that George must have left a will that would prove James not to be a beneficiary. Three years later one was found in the curtain folds of George's death bed by a servant called Jessie Watson. The case was taken to the Court of Session where Lord Mackenzie found it to be genuine, but was unanimously overruled by the First Division judges who had suspicions such as why did George More place the will in such a strange place and why did it remain undiscovered for so long? It was also noted that the will was dated on a Sunday, but More had been a member of the Original Secession Church, a particularly strict sect whose followers would not have undertaken such a task on the Sabbath. James was a very benevolent man. He founded the Monkrigg Benevolent Fund for aged and poor people and hundreds were benefited to the extent of £5 per person per year. £300 was given to the Town Council to build a school in his memory. It was decided to name the school after John Knox and More's bequest was used to found a bursary. When the house was put up for sale in 1947 it had four public rooms, a billiard room, eight bedrooms, four dressing rooms and three bathrooms. In addition it also came with offices, fruit and vegetable gardens and 200 acres of cultivated arable land. It was purchased by the Manclark family. They changed aspects of the house's interior, but the B-listed exterior remained untouched.

The seeds of Neilson Park were sown in 1897 when George Neilson of Bellevue, Haddington, died. His will stipulated that some monies from his estate should be used to build a memorial that would benefit the town and the surrounding area, and that the memorial should never be handed over to the control of the council. His trustees resolved to create a park and recreation area, and to this end purchased the land known as Mylne's Park for £5,500. In the grounds were football and cricket pitches, a pavilion, a greenhouse and a potting shed. Twenty tons of iron were used by John Nisbet, a blacksmith based in Lodge Street, to create 20,000 railings and decorative gates, although these were all removed during the Second World War. It was to be formally opened by Lord Wemyss in June 1910, but first the death of Edward VII and then an accident suffered by Lord Wemyss caused its opening to be delayed. The public were, however, allowed access. The park is shown here soon after opening. By 1948 the money from his estate was almost spent and, contrary to Neilson's wishes, his bequest to the town was passed to the Town Council who could ensure its ongoing maintenance.

The Nungate Bridge dates from the thirteenth century. The nineteen mason marks that adorn its stonework attest to a troubled past when repairs were commonplace. It is over 100 feet long and its original steep ends made it virtually impossible for loaded carts to use it as a crossing point. In many cases those wishing to cross would be forced to do so via the nearby ford, shown opposite. Both photographs were taken around 1905. On the far left of the picture of the bridge can be seen the public washhouse, known as the 'steamie', while in the photograph of the ford the white building is the abattoir which was demolished in 1975.

The second of Haddington's bridges was called the Gimmers Mills Bridge. Although a private bridge, the public were allowed to use it. It is believed to have been built around the middle of the nineteenth century, but by the time this photograph was taken in 1895 it was in a state of serious disrepair. Worried by this, local businessman Alexander Hogarth, who owned the mill (it was soon repurchased by Montgomerie and Co.), proposed to replace it with a steel structure affixed to the existing stone piers. He argued that if the monies came from the public purse then the public could use it, but if he had to pay for it himself it would remain private and used only by mill traffic. Hogarth estimated that the total cost would be around £1,000. Despite the concerns about the old bridge many were opposed to building a new one. Did the town have enough money? Would the town benefit from a new bridge or was it simply being built to benefit the mill owners? The Town Council did take the scheme on board and three years later the plans were drawn up.

At the same time an accident on the old bridge led to its partial collapse. Thirty-three feet of its side was destroyed when a horse and cart crashed through it and fell into the river below. The horse later died. Speed, however, was obviously not of the essence and it took a further three years before the final pier of the old bridge was demolished. The new Victoria Bridge, eventually built a little way to the south of the Gimmers Mills Bridge, was partly paid for by subscription and the subscribers ranged from the great and the good (the Earl of Haddington, A.J. Balfour MP and R.B. Haldane MP), to local worthies (Dr Martine, Charles Bruce and D. & J. Croal) and the common people of the town. The structure was opened in 1900 having cost £9,237 to build. Behind the bridge are Gimmers Mills on the left and the Bermaline Mill on the right.

The River Tyne rises in Midlothian and winds its way eastwards towards the sea. On the way it meanders through Haddington, creating a natural barrier between the western end of the town and Nungate. A writer in 1913 complained that although the town was smoke and bustle free, the river was covered with 'a horrid scum' due to domestic sewage. This seemed to have a positive effect on the size of the trout and resulted in them often being double the size of those in cleaner waters. A three-pounder was not uncommon.

Despite one poet calling it the 'gentle Tyne', the River Tyne has occasionally flooded its banks throughout the centuries. In 1358 the Nungate was swept away by high waters. Further floods occurred in 1421, 1775 and 1846, although it is likely that there were many others in between. The photograph on the left shows the bottom of High Street during a flood, probably around 1931. The photograph below shows the river's overflowing banks at the Nungate Bridge. One of the worst floods in recent memory took place on 12/13 August 1948. The flooded area stretched from the Town House to Amisfield Park, much being under several feet of water. Boats from North Berwick were used to rescue the stranded and 50 families were registered homeless. The aftermath saw £950,000 being paid out in compensation.

The place of John Knox's birth has been a contentious issue through the years. Was he born in Gifford, Morham, or Giffordgate in Nungate? The majority favour Giffordgate, shown on the front cover. But wherever he was born his name is well remembered in Haddington, for example, with Knox Court, Knox Place, the Knox Tree, and the Knox Institute. Haddington is known to have had a school before 1378, when a payment of £3 15*s* 2*d* was made to the town's schoolmaster by Robert II. In later years the town's first grammar school was attended by Knox, and it was he, ironically, who was indirectly responsible for the hiring of the town's first Protestant schoolmaster, Robert Dormont, in 1559. A number of other schools, both public and private, were founded in the following centuries. It was in 1879 that the Knox Institute opened its doors for the first time, although the formal opening, by Arthur J. Balfour MP, took place in January of the following year. It combined all the town's higher grade schools under one roof. Above the main entrance, just visible in this picture, stands a statue of Knox, gifted by the Misses Turnbull of Aberlady and sculpted by D.W. Stevenson. This photograph was taken around 1908, before the clock was added. In 1938 a new building, Knox Academy, was erected at Meadow Park and the students moved there. The institute was converted into sheltered housing in 1985.

On the eastern side of the River Tyne sits Nungate, a suburb of Haddington whose name is derived from the nuns who worked at St Martin's Church. The church is visible in the background of this photograph. The inhabitants of Haddington and Nungate saw themselves as distinct communities. Trouble between youths was not unknown, and one nineteenth-century cry from the Haddington side went:

'Ye Nungate cuds, cock up yer fuds
An' let the Haddingtons bye;
We'll drive ye east wi' bickering thuds,
Until ye're tired and dune glad lye.'

Amisfield House was designed by Isaac Ware and built of red freestone around 1755. The history of the grounds extend back further than this however. They were originally known as Newmilns and in 1681 Colonel Sir James Stanfield, one of Cromwell's officers, opened a fine woollen cloth manufactory in the grounds. The business declined after Stanfield was reputedly murdered. It was said that his body bled when a suspect, his son, touched it (a sure sign that he was guilty of murder) and he was hanged in Edinburgh for the crime, then beheaded, and his head was 'spiked' at Haddington. The Colonel's ghost reputedly still haunts the well in the grounds. The estate was later purchased by Francis Charteris, and it was he who changed the name to Amisfield. Charteris was a card cheat, loan shark and rapist, and his deeds were so infamous that in the literature of the day he was equated with the devil. Charteris was well aware of the error of his ways and on his deathbed he promised £30,000 to anyone who could prove that hell did not exist. At his funeral in Dalkeith in 1732, rioters tried to tear his body from its coffin and once this was lowered into the ground it was covered with dead animals. His descendants built the house shown here and filled it with fine

rt. By 1792 its walls were adorned with paintings by Annibal Caracci, Pompeio, Murillo and Rubens. During the Great War the house served as a military raining camp for the 1st Regiment of the Lothians and Border Horse and the 4th (Res.) Battalion Royal Scots. The officers were barracked in the house and the ordinary soldiers in huts in the grounds. The soldier in the tin helmet, photographed around the time of the Great War, is Private R.F. Scott, No. 63477, of B Company, 4th (Res.) Battalion Royal Scots and probably a native of St Andrews. The regiment never made its way to the front. In 1928 the house was purchased by Richard Baillie & Sons of Pencaitland. They demolished it and some of the stone was used to build the Vert Memorial Hospital, Longniddry Golf Club House and Preston Lodge High School. The grounds were used as a military compound during the Second World War, housing Polish troops and later German and Ukranian prisoners of war. They worked on local farms and market gardens and this led to a number of friendships striking up between locals and prisoners, several of which lasted beyond the prisoners' repatriation to their homeland. The grounds have also been used on and off by Haddington Golf Club since 1865.

)ne could be forgiven for thinking that Colstoun House was uilt in the Victorian era, but the truth is that centuries of uilding work have transformed this thirteenth century tructure from 'a small, square tower.' Its long history has also vitnessed more than its fair share of tragedy. In 1270 the Laird f Colstoun married the daughter of Hugo de Gifford, Lord of 'ester. Unable to afford a dowry, Gifford presented his laughter with a pear, telling her that the success and future of he family would go hand in hand with its fate. It allegedly emained intact for 400 years, but stories of what happened ext vary. Some say Lady Elizabeth M'Kenzie, wife of George roun, bit into the pear. Others tell that she only dreamt of loing so. Whatever the true story, misfortune soon befell the amily. George Broun's gambling saw the family lose its farms t Newhall, while Elizabeth could not bear George a son and eir. George was forced to sell his remaining lands to his rother Robert. Robert had two sons, thus ensuring the family ine, but one day, on crossing the Colstoun Water, Robert's 'arriage overturned and he and his sons drowned. Nearly 200 'ears later a portrait of Lady Elizabeth, the cause of this upposed misfortune, was found in an attic in the house, torn rom its frame and facing a wall. But tragedy for the family did ot end there. In 1907 Lady Edith Broun-Lindsay showed some riends the pear (which at that time was described as 'about the ize of a walnut, of a dark mahogany colour') and soon after a ire, starting in the attic, destroyed part of the house, which had o be rebuilt. The photograph on the left probably shows the ftermath of that event. The pear still survives, housed in a ilver casket, viewed only by family members, and touched by one. During and after the Second World War Colstoun ontinued to be the home of the Broun-Lindsay family. Captain C.G. Broun-Lindsay died in 1989, and his wife and daughter ontinued to reside there. The house was reduced in size etween 1990 and 1992 and a large number of antiques were old through Sotheby's. The portrait of Duleep Singh by George Beechey, for example, visible on the far wall in the interior hotograph, was estimated to sell at $40,000 to $60,000.

Corridor, Colstoun House, Haddington

Alderston House, situated one mile to the north west of Haddington, was built around 1788 and for a time was called Smeaton Park. Over the next 131 years it had a number of owners including Robert Hay, Captain Tod, Robert Steuart of Calcutta, James Aitchison, and Mr Cossar Mackenzie. From 1919 it was derelict, but in 1925 it was purchased by the Scottish National Benevolent Association for use as a convalescent home for the Scottish Rural Workers' Association's male members, who were admitted free of charge for as long as was medically recommended. At this time the house was situated in 40 acres of land and had 21 bedrooms, three bathrooms, electric light, central heating, an electricity-generating plant, a billiard room, a piano, an organ, a gramophone and a wireless. After 1950 parts were purchased by the NHS and served as Roodlands Hospital's Nurses' Training School and Nurses' Home. Purchased by Lothian Regional Council in 1975 to house their water and drainage department, it was used from 1984 to train those on the government's Youth Training Scheme (YTS). However, it could have had a very different recent history, if, as some members of the council proposed, its basement had been turned into an Emergency Control Centre that would have been used in the event of a nuclear war. With proposed costs of £45,000 it was voted against, with Labour councillor Neil Lindsay calling it a 'monumental charade'. It currently serves as a Centre for Lifelong Learning and in its first term 550 students took courses on topics such as Spanish, a 'Beginner's Guide to Wine', and book-keeping.

Half a mile south of Haddington once sat the impressive Clerkington House. Part of the original house was swept away in the flood of 1775. Twenty years later it was purchased by Alexander Houstoun, governor of Grenada in the West Indies. This was the beginning of a relationship between the Houstouns and the house that would last into the twentieth century. It had 42 rooms and the lavishness of these is reflected in those who chose to rent or visit. In 1862 Charles Lawson, Lord Provost of Edinburgh, spent a season there and in 1876 it played host to Prince Arthur, Duke of Connaught. In the twentieth century the house was purchased by the Ford family. When Mrs Ford died in the early 1930s the house passed to her son Ludovic, the famous racing driver. During the Second World War, it served as the headquarters of No. 405 Searchlight Company of the 4th/5th Battalion, The Queen's Royal Scots (later the 52nd Searchlight Regiment). In 1951 Ford sold the house with the upset price being £3,750. The new owner intended to turn it into flats. By 1966, however, it was in a state of serious disrepair with smashed windows, rotting doors, damaged plaster and loose chimney pots. Although it was a listed building its poor condition was such that East Lothian Planning Committee allowed it to be condemned.

Lying three miles to the south of Haddington is the small rural village of Bolton. The town has a unique place in Scotland's history as for many years it was the home of Scotland's oldest-surviving road vehicle – the Bolton Hearse. The hearse was purchased by the heritors of the parish in 1783 for the sum of £39 13*s* 2*d*, although the undercarriage probably dates from at least 100 years earlier. If two horses were used to transport the dead the cost was 8*s* for the first mile and 9*s* thereafter. If four horses were used the fee would rise by 2*s* and 3*s* respectively. It was last used in 1843, but before its final journey it had had at least one famous occupant – Robert Burns's mother. It sat unused in the old coachhouse of Bolton Churchyard until 1925 when it was finally restored to its full glory at Kennedy and Co., coachbuilders of Haddington. Along the hearse's sides are symbols (a skull and hour glass) and inscriptions ('Memento Mori' and 'Tempus Fugit'). The hearse is now on view as one of the great treasures of the Museum of Scotland in Edinburgh. This photograph shows it just prior to restoration.

One and a half miles south of Haddington lies one of Scotland's finest country houses – Lennoxlove. Built in the fifteenth century it was known as Lethington Tower until the end of the 1600s. Perhaps the house's most colourful and adventurous owner was the fourteenth Duke of Hamilton, who purchased it for £4,000 in 1946. By this time he was already considered a hero as, in 1932, he was the first person to fly over Mount Everest as chief pilot of the Mount Everest Flight Expedition. During the Second World War Rudolph Hess attempted to fly to meet him to broker a peace deal between Germany and Britain. The duke died at Lennoxlove in 1973 and, appropriately, his eldest son scattered his ashes over the estate from the air. In 1997 the house suffered a fire, but was successfully restored.

As East Lothian is an area which for centuries has been an agricultural heartland, several small communities have been founded in the hinterland of the larger towns. Close to Haddington, for example, are Liberty Hall and Samuelston Loanhead. The Liberty Hall houses were built around 1826. Many of the houses in these two photographs, both taken just prior to the Great War, have been demolished.

SAMUELSTON LOANHEAD, HADDINGTON.

Cistercian monks were active in Scotland by the mid-twelfth century when abbeys were built at Melrose and Newbattle. The Sancta Maria Abbey at Nunraw, near Haddington, was founded by monks from Roscrea, Ireland, in 1946. Work began on the building shown in the background of this picture in 1952, and it was finally finished in 1969. It cost £150,000 to build, but would have cost much more had it not been for the volunteers who travelled each year to help erect it. The old dormitories were replaced by single rooms and at the house's opening Abbot Samuel Mulcahy, its 'spiritual and temporal head', joked that 'today men are not so handy at resisting snoring.' The men rise at 3.15 a.m. and for the following four hours spend time in prayer, community Mass and private prayer. At 7.30 a.m. work begins on the farm, ensuring the monks' livelihood is derived mainly from 'manual labour, agriculture and the rearing of cattle.' In 1969 the abbey was surrounded by 500 acres of arable land upon which there were 470 sheep, 640 lambs, 150 cattle and 200 poultry. Although decision taking rests with the Abbot, the emphasis is on democracy, with the community of monks being consulted before any decisions are finalised. The order also opens its doors to those in need of aid, and Robert Louis Stevenson was one of those who took advantage of the order's kindliness at a monastery in France.